THE BOSS

THE BOSS
VICTORIA CHANG

MᶜSWEENEY'S
POETRY SERIES

McSWEENEY'S

SAN FRANCISCO

www.mcsweeneys.net

The McSweeney's Poetry Series is edited by Dominic Luxford and Jesse Nathan.

The editors wish to thank assistant editor Rachel Z. Arndt, editorial interns
Greg J. Griffith, Alex Morris, and Jasmine Dreame Wagner, and copyeditor Britta Ameel.

ISBN: 978-1-938073-58-8

Printed in Michigan by Thomson-Shore.

TABLE OF CONTENTS

I ONCE WAS A CHILD

I once was a child am a child am someone's child
      not my mother's not my father's the boss
    gave us special treatment treatment for something
        special a lollipop or a sticker glitter from the

toy box the better we did the better the plastic prize made
      in China one year everyone got a spinning top
    one year everyone got a tap on their shoulders
        one year everyone was fired everyone

fired but me one year we all lost our words one year
      my father lost his words to a stroke
    a stroke of bad luck stuck his words
        used to be so worldly his words fired

him let him go without notice can they do that
      can she do that yes she can in this land she can
    once we sang songs around a piano *this land is your land*
        this land is my land in this land someone always

owns the land in this land someone who owns
      the land owns the buildings on the land owns
    the people in the buildings unless an earthquake
        sucks the land in like a long noodle

TODAY IS THE BOSS

Today is the boss the boss is today the day shines
        her white teeth today is the boss
    the boss gives us tokens to take a bus
        to a restaurant to bus her table she

breaks our plates our dirty plates break when thrown
        I sit cross-legged on the floor to do pilates to
    plot with my colleagues to glue the plates together again
        up in the sky a bird keeps flying in

the shape of a cross the shadow of my body is a cross
        it never leaves me it never helps me only at night
    on my back we come together briefly the next day the boss
        takes a bus and drives over us over our

plates again and again the boss pretends to glue us after
        she breaks us we try to glue ourselves
    Elmer's allows us to emerge as a different person I have
        a piece of someone else's saucer as my heart

WE ARE HIGH PERFORMERS

We are high performers not normal but high performers
we perform things make papers smell like
perfume we are *highly creative unusually industrious*
exceptionally conscientious diligent intelligent

we are high performers former high hopers on a high wire
balancing a ream of paper on our heads
no net under us just the boss with her arms crossed
in a knot glasses fogged we think

she is smiling yes the boss is definitely smiling she has
finally found a vein on her wrist that smells of oil
we plug away despite the plagues in other countries
we are still in awe of the boss and

the law and all the dollars the doll I once had is now my
daughter's doll she will dream of balls and
gowns and sparkly towns when should I tell her all the
towns are falling down

MY FATHER SAYS

My father says the wrong things I say the wrong things
     my father thinks he is 42 not 69 my father
  was born in 1942 my father thinks his address
     is 1942 my father sits in a hospital

he thinks the year is 1942 that I am 1942 years old that his
     knee is 1942 he thinks his name is 1942
  he says he is in the hospital because of *weight* or maybe
     he means *wait* or *lean* maybe he means

he leaned on the toilet he was fixing and fell down
     he doesn't know where his nose is but he
  knows 1942 when I was 19 I wanted to be a doctor
     in a few years I will be 42 and I will

be afraid of doctors I can no longer think of the right
     words to say my words come out
  of my mouth twisted turned in spirals like a dancer
     wrapping her leg around a pole

on some days the boss takes our 1942 and turns it
     into 2491 on other days she turns it into
  1429 and on the worst days she smiles at us
     and her smile looks like a 9 turned

on its side with a cat's tongue sticking out when asked
     to close his eyes my father points
  to the white stack of papers when asked if his name
     is Adam he points to the papers as if

to say ask the papers don't ask me he no longer knows
that a Chinese man from Taiwan can't
possibly be named Adam or Bill or Bob or John
or Gus maybe now he thinks

a Chinese man from Taiwan can be a CEO can be
a boss in America maybe now
he thinks his name is Adam maybe that is
why he named me Victoria

EDWARD HOPPER'S *OFFICE AT NIGHT*

The boss is sitting at the desk the boss doesn't look
       at her the boss is waiting for the black telephone
to ring she also waits for a ring from the boss he is
       waiting for the files from her

her blue dress like a reused file folder around
       her body her hands tight around the files
the filing cabinet might eat her might take her hand off
       the boss might eat her the boss

wants her but the boss wants money more just a little bit
       more the boss always seems to want
the money a bit more the boss doesn't hear
       there are taxis outside waiting

for all the women down on the street across the street
       a boss prepares for bed another boss above him
in apartment X rotates a Q-tip in his ear before sex
       despite instructions on the box we took

my father out of the paper the living will the letters
       with their little capes will leave the paper
who will take care of my children later who will take care
       of my father the will will take care

of no one a piece of paper cannot take care of anyone I
       cannot take care of everyone on some nights
I wake in a panic and can't tell if I am dead or alive
       this year I dye my hair so I won't have to die

THE BOSS IS NOT POETIC

The boss is not poetic writing about the boss is not poetic
a corporate pencil doesn't gallop
dactyls one foot two feet six feet seven the boss
only has two feet the rain taps its

trimeters all over my roof the boss can only jump up and
down in one spot the boss cannot do the
splits the rain splits into pieces the rain slants into
my face into my eyes that are not really

slanted the boss only rhymes with *cross* and *loss*
poem rhymes with *palindrome* and *loam* a desk is
not poetic either it has four sides hard and stiff a
Herman Miller chair loses question marks

through its holes as it holds a Herman or a Miller one day
I watch a shrill pelican dive straight down into
the water a waiter brings us fish on a plate a pelican
swallows a fish whole a pelican is the boss

with its endless office of sky I could stand on the pier
the whole day and peer at the pelicans that fall
from the sky with their briefcases of fish in their
oily grey suits and shined black shoes

THE BOSS RISES

The boss rises up the boss keeps her job
        the boss is safe the workers are not
    the boss smiles the boss files the boss
        throws pennies at the workers

the boss rises up higher and higher the boss's
        head is the balloon getting bigger
    and bigger it gets harder and harder to hold
        on the workers do good work

the boss goes higher towards the sky's work
        higher and higher she shakes
    her legs tries to shake the workers
        off little bugs with little bags

of personal belongings in plastic bins like the Bens
        and Tims and their friends we
    can be bosses too can hold the cross but
        there is a cost

I DRIVE UP HILLS

I drive up hills to see the tops of other people's heads
at the top I can't read books at the top
I can't watch my own children at the top I am
dumb I am numb at the top

but still I want to go to the top because that's where
a boss sits a boss has fits at the top gives
tips at the top a boss gets into tip-top shape
on the way up yesterday I met a boss

who asked his people how they felt once I
met a boss who knelt as he bused
tables who helped his people without his arms
on his hips my father wanted me

to be a boss who can fire up people
who can fire people my father used to
circle English words he didn't know with a
red pen now his books drip red now

his books have locks he has an aphasia workbook
he asks my four-year-old to help when I
ask him the name of his old boss
he says his own name

THERE IS ONLY ONE

There is only one I am not the one
        who won being the one means you
    can power more than one more than two
        three ten one guard can power

a white field of naked prisoners without
        anything but a gun the prisoners stand
    in a line they have a choice but they have
        no choice when the plane is

hijacked Jack in 14D is still delighting that he
        is above the clouds better than
    the clouds he has spent his life looking up
        but when the man in 13E says

to put their hands on their heads he will stop
        watching Oprah his body will tense
    up he will hear opera in his ears he will
        suddenly forget he is one

of hundreds and there is only one hijacker
        his future tense will listen to
    13E even as he falls and his face is pressed
        on the plane's plain carpet

EDWARD HOPPER'S *CHAIR CAR*

Everything green everything grown and aglow
    everything looks sour like a green
    apple sucker the woman reading a book doesn't
    look like a sucker but she doesn't

look like a boss either doesn't look cross doesn't cross
    her legs the woman across from her looks
    like a boss she wears a red blur she looks at
    the woman reading with the stare

of a boss a *what-are-you-doing* stare the woman reading
    like a worker unaware of the glare
    unaware of someone writing an algorithm to
    read her emails the woman with the

hat and the man cannot be bosses they look down look
    away he looks at a white door without
    handles and realizes there's no way out she is
    about to get a demotion passed

over because of her emotion even
    the chairs position themselves so they
    can look the most lost at the next stop so they can
    shiver at the touch of a boss

I ONLY KNEW DICTATORS

I only knew dictators I loved the unilateral directions
      the high diction my father sat
   in his office dictating his thoughts about
        meetings with bosses my father dictated

to me to eat tomatoes my father was dictated to
      by his boss the bush blooms flowers
   each spring pink ones open then the blooms fall
      the bush resumes being a bush

a boss changes seasonally too a boss can turn into
      a dictator and back again the boss sees
   everything we play hide and seek with
      the boss but she always finds

us we always hide in the same place
      my office faces the boss's office but our
   doors don't align some days when I can no longer
      lie I shut my door and cry the rain

always gives me away when I play hide and seek
      with my two-year-old she lies
   on the ground and covers her face she thinks
      I can't see her

THE BOSS HAS A FATHER

The boss has a father further than my father the boss
        doesn't speak to her father or her mother the boss
    doesn't speak to others the boss smothers the boss
            hovers over and under and within

emails the boss rewrites emails the boss writes
        mysteries the boss writes endings my father
    writes his name on the aphasia workbook writes
            my name calls my name calls me

my sister *Debbie* everyone is *Debbie* my daughters are
        Debbie every Debbie must be heavy must be
    ready to hear my father call them all day call
            them *Debbie* his favorite daughter

THE BOSS TELLS ME

The boss tells me of the billionaire who likes me
      who likes my work again this year
   this year I am safe for another year I can stand by
      for another year I can align

myself with the bystanders who have different
      standards for another year I can mortgage my heart
   in monthly installments for another year I can fill
      my garage with scooters and things

with motors like Mona at the end of the hall with
      her loan and home and college bills who never
   sees anything in the office never seems to hear
      anything in the office but her own

heartbeat her own term sheet for another year
      when asked about Mary or Tom or Larry I too
   can say I never saw anything never saw the boss
      wind them up and point them towards the

edge of the roof before Mary went over the
      edge I threw down a pillow in the shape of a
   pet and hoped it landed under her I didn't stay long
      enough to see what happened

THE BOSS IS BACK

The boss is back from the hospital is hospitable then
                    hostile the boss gave birth the boss
          lay still on a bed to rest to bedrest to rest
                    the baby girl on the bed

each morning I lay my case to rest but there's no jury no
                    fury I lay my baby on the bed I sponge
          her I wonder whether the boss feels what I feel
                    for my baby a heel on a cheek

doesn't always mean love the boss kicks up her heels
                    her eyes empty and eerie like a fish's eyes
          we are weary we are wary of the boss we
                    sleep standing up but so

does the boss miles and miles under the sea even the fish
                    don't sleep they can hear the helicopters
          carrying soldiers going back and forth
                    and back and forth

EDWARD HOPPER'S *NEW YORK OFFICE*

Maybe the letter isn't from a lover the letter is a layoff letter
a lay-aside letter a lay-into letter maybe the
letter says you are an employee of me so I certainly
expect you to come to the meeting

about me my two-year-old says *me don't have candy*
me me me my tooth hurts my foot hurts *me have*
boo-boo here and here and here and here
I can never see them these boo-boos

cannot see anything maybe her letter is a DMV letter telling
her to pay the registration fee the license fee the
weight fee the special plate fee the city county
state fees the owner responsibility fee the smog

abatement fee maybe if the DMV didn't have so
many fees the woman would be free to work in a
different building with a different window in a
different city for a different boss

THE BOSS'S CHRISTMAS CARD

The boss's Christmas card is red her children
    are well-fed one year after firing
someone she went home she went to a field or
    a backyard or somewhere with trees

and thistle and grass she went home and lifted
    the boy into her arms and swung him
in circles in circles he went and her glasses fell
    a little and the boy fell a little the boy

grabbed her face and she laughed and someone
    froze them in a picture she sat down she sat us
down each day she sat the employee down to fire
    him but some photographer watched

her through a small rectangle and knew what her red
    eyes meant each year she fired someone
kind someone competent with a letter all through
    the winter we watched her

where were the bosses to watch her does a tree
    mind that it can never move does a tree
mood can a mind ever change can a certain
    kind of mind ever kind

THE BOSS HAS GREY HAIR

The boss has grey hair the boss's hair has greyed down
        from the roots now everyone is rooting for
    the worker but nothing takes root all is grey everything
        is changing everything is unchanged

a paddle striking water changes something
        something moves over water but the water
    remains water and the paddle a paddle HR is
        the water HR wants to keep its job HR

fills in the indentations the paddle makes the
        paddle makes HR work HR is always sweating is
    always wetting itself HR is not very human is a
        nervous artificial heart aware that it might

stop beating the boss has grey hair now the only thing
        that changes HR doesn't change the square
    root of 4 remains 2 just as the square root of
        the boss is always the boss

WE CAN'T SAY ANYTHING

We can't say anything need the numbers need
      the blue paper that represents green
    paper that represents the field of poplars bi-monthly
        to buy things DVDs DVRs RVs numbers

calculators in our dreams IRAs press down on our
      401(k) roofs the *click click click* of numbers
    in our dreams not a bird pecking for birdseeds
        but pecking for 401(k)s even the birds

can't remember when the sky wasn't stippled green
      even my father who can't remember much
    remembers there are passwords but he can't
        remember his passwords can't get past

his words can't figure out what the pass is for can't
      access his accounts can't remember
    ass-kissing for his large accounts can't account
        for himself can no longer count

EDWARD HOPPER'S *OFFICE AT NIGHT*

Maybe the woman in the blue dress is the boss
        maybe the man leaning over the paper
    is not the boss maybe the man is filling out
            an application for employment maybe

the woman for her enjoyment came into
        the office to check on the man to make
    sure he is still working before she leaves
            for the night before she leaves

to meet her boss for drinks maybe the woman is
        checking on his work footing his numbers
    his one foot barely shows under the table the
            other hides in a shadow when

things go wrong whose fault is it everyone wants
        to know who started the fights in the office
    some nights I hear my two-year-old fighting
            with someone in her crib she is bossing

someone around *no no no bad that's mine you don't take*
        mine I wonder if she will be a future boss
    in the office with the green carpet with the
            blood-red stains bossing around

the man who can't get his numbers to foot on other
        nights I hear her singing *happy birthday to*
    me happy birthday to me she is already celebrating
            herself she will be the perfect boss

THE BOSS WOULD LIKE TO SEE

The boss would like to see us not in person
        but would like to see us do something
      better the boss would like to see us see ourselves
            differently would like to see if

we can do something one way her way that way
        I take out the sign and turn the arrow
      the other way another one comes in is hired to see
            if something can be executed to see if

others can be muted if someone can be
        refuted looted electrocuted another one
      comes in and turns around and walks out on the way
            out another one looks at us calls us

brave the group is scared the group no longer wants
        to be groped the group scores me strokes
      me scores points by being silent the boss's hair
            looks like lint it turns grey then

greyer her hair hugs me envies me for being
        brave not a slave for being free
      of the boss my eyebrows for being shaped
            like birds that think they can fly away

I ONCE HAD A GOOD BOSS

I once had a good boss a National Guard kind of boss
        soft as a flag tough as a pole I once had a
    good boss a god boss who played me like
           a good bass plucked all my strings now

my good boss is gone is a goner boss is a no-longer-
        mine boss is someone else's boss I once
    had a good boss but didn't know he was a good boss
        until I met my new boss my

good boss called me V the letter looks like a check mark
        he checked me off each day with a soft
    charcoal pencil he said *V* with such kindness the way
        a cement sidewalk lifts itself up slowly year

after year for ficus roots if only I could hug
        my once-good boss bug him each day once again
    exceed his expectations set my objectives around his
        goals be his shoal but it is too late I am

old now the land is cold now the owl on some nights opens
        my window and waits for me to wake
    in a wet sweat its gold eyes staring at me like
        two ticking clocks

EDWARD HOPPER'S *AUTOMAT*

The woman in the automat must work must
    have a boss must walk
  to work two legs red with heat two legs
      pressed into each other as if one

depended on the other the woman in the automat
    takes one glove off to hold
  the cup to shake the hand of a boss one hand
    free she looks down at the circle

on the table looks down at the round reflection
    of circular lights her boss circulates
  memos her boss is the circle the circumference
    circles her each day like a minnow

her boss multiplies into millions of circles the boss
    multiplies her zeroes the boss bonuses
  pro bonos her views her views collect
    in the air ascend to space collide

with stars lie to the moon for anyone to listen
    punching anything in sight on some nights
  the moon speaks up because it knows it will still
    have a job on some nights the moon

shines its white mane on everything
    I've ever done wrong I can't bear
  to look at the light the blank doe eye
    like a shadow I can't shake

THE BOSS WEARS A WHITE VEST

The boss wears a white vest a white face through
      the hole of a 700-fill-power vest
    the boss keeps her body heat in the down vest
      I want to power down the boss

the boss keeps her power the boss's new boss
      doesn't like her the boss's old boss doesn't
    like her it doesn't matter the boss keeps us in her
      hand warmer pockets her pockets

filled with treats in the shapes of imported hearts
      we are all imported from somewhere the boss
    talks about our heritage her adage starts with
      I think you are I think my age is

four my cage is made of a tear-resistant
      nylon shell my four-year-old daughter still
    listens to me I am the boss and I like it I
      see why the boss likes it

I USED TO MY FATHER USED TO

I used to my father used to I used to
        sit in a living room with my mother's
thousand miniature teapots I used to
        talk to my father about

letters AAPL GOOG YHOO what do they
        do what do they look like to him now
goo-goo ga-ga ooh-ooh ah-ah I ask him what
        his password is he says *Gmail*

he says mail is in the box he says *www.gmail.com*
        I ask for the password he says
www.gmail.com he looks it up his brain
        locks up he wonders what a

password is letters numbers symbols
        dumbbells something he needs to get
something to get into something in order
        to get something else he used

to be free used to need used to want
        more of something of some
secret thing he used to need to know
        what he had I need a password

into a past a pasture into my father into
        his brain I used to speak to my father
my father used to speak I used to
        speak up

THE BOSS WEARS WRIST GUARDS

The boss wears wrist guards I risk carpal tunnel without
        them can't see anything but her fingers
    love line hidden justice line hidden the heart line leaks
        out the end of it sneaks out of the guard

the black guard covers the heart line is it wavy is it long and
        curvy broken is it broken mine touches my life
    line my heart breaks easily my daughter's heart line
        begins below the middle finger she is

selfish please don't be a selfish boss please be a boss please
        be selfish the middle finger is the longest the
    middle is used by those without power who want it but
        the fingers are stuck together once

a neighbor lost his middle finger while fixing a
        lawn mower no longer able to flip someone off the
    middle finger does not resemble a bird the bird is
        something with power the bird can fly away

EDWARD HOPPER'S *OFFICE IN A SMALL CITY*

The man could be the boss or could
        have a boss the man is not working
    should be working should be making
        profits not in fits but constantly

the man looks out over the yellow building over
        everything he must be the boss must
    be someone significant someone constant
        above everything maybe the man is

deciding who to hire fire who to layoff who
        to slay with a fire maybe he is deciding
    who is the best liar to hire but the man
        doesn't smile doesn't look at the people

walking in the street or the cars honking below
        the man sits and stares at the shapes
    of vents on the roof of a building rearranging
        them people are just shapes a circle

for a head rectangles for the body arms
        and legs this man's head over
    this woman's body this woman's head with
        another man's legs maybe the man

is looking at the horizon wondering why a plane
        in the sky is pointed downward towards
    the morning glories the okra or the
        building with five sides

SOME DAYS ONE DAY

Some days one day every day I am over like the
        plover or the roses but nothing seasonal the rose
    gets to hide in a bud stroke noses spike others
        some days I want to speak to others

confess how much I hate computers with their
        gaudy square teeth that hurt people with their
    fangs their words but only *thank you please sincerely* come
        out of my mouth my lips with

their false color and old etchings how tiresome to spend
        a lifetime buttoning things how I wish to
    unbutton the moon from the tar sky and stick my
        tongue out at the neutral mute

I once had a book called *Nobody's Perfect* but
        some people are perfect so each night
    I sew my daughter's bear over and over her
        lucky bear loved for its nubs and

flubs my blood has nowhere to go trapped in this
        cavity circling and reassuring itself chasing
    itself until one day it will rush out and
        never look back

THE BOSS LOOKS OVER US

The boss looks over us the boss likes us the boss
        irks us hurts us the boss smiles
    at us smirks at us the boss lies to us confirms
        her offer of employment the boss

gives us provides us deploys us the boss
        accommodates us no animus no
animal no nitpick she picked us and her and
        her to knit together we tried to

knit my father back together
        starting with *I am Victoria I am*
    your daughter you have two daughters I am I can
        I have to be knitted back together

I am a flaw *a burst of passion or a passing wind*
        in an office a burst of passion can
only lead to the door out the door down
        the stairs through another door into

the passionate wind where there once used to sit
        a metal bull near a fountain with a gold sphere
    and people eating lunch people eating benches people
        covered with lungs and dust

THERE ARE TWO WAYS

There are two ways maybe four there are
　　　　two ways of seeing one way maybe
　　　　not our way maybe the boss's way maybe the boss
　　　　　　is right maybe we are wrought

wrong ruined maybe the boss knows
　　　　the boss is god is good and we are
　　　　made to be maids maybe the boss knows
　　　　　　why the storm makes the sky look

like a toilet flushing why the twisting sky today
　　　　looks like someone like us should
　　　　mop it up why a twister in the sky mistakes
　　　　　　a cross on a steeple for an X to

hit why a town named Joplin has rain like javelins
　　　　and humans scattering why
　　　　the boy was sucked right out of
　　　　　　the roof like a root

THE BOSS HAS A BAND OF PEOPLE

The boss has a band of people around her the way
        a band bends around her finger the boss's
husband calls her a Rottweiler *a watchdog a powerful*
           breed with guarding instincts and strong desire

to control one day at a park I watched a Rottweiler chase
        a ball chase after me I ran the Rottweiler
ran I jumped into the water the Rottweiler
          swam its mouth open forty-two rotting

teeth tongue out I jumped from the water looked
        at my own wagging tail my Rottweiler topcoat
of black the boss behind me clothes dripping forehead
          wrinkles panting smiling putting her fogged

glasses back on once there were films where people
        didn't speak and we wanted nothing more
even our hearts try to get bigger a hundred
          thousand times each day

EDWARD HOPPER'S *NEW YORK OFFICE*

Her boss is somewhere where is her boss
  she holds a letter almost blue could be
 blown away but there's no window if her world had
   wind she would be happy she could blow

away her face tight too afraid to open the letter to
  let her learn how she can be better why
 someone no longer wants her the boss said
   I have something for you have something

like a box or a present for me for someone that used
  to be but no box no present nothing with
 ribbons or pink or an envelope of sequins shaped
   like hearts the boss said *I have something*

for you I have something to return to you I
  opened the box saw my head a butterfly
 lands on my stump if you subtract
   its wings it looks like a fly if you

subtract my head I am nothing parts of
  me in a pile with other parts in a ditch
 in any countryside during any war from
   afar it looks like we are hugging

MY FATHER USED TO BE SELFISH

My father used to be selfish he used to like fish
        now he can't identify fish I wish
    I were selfish I used to be selfish on some days
            I think how easy to sell fish on a boat

in another ocean shucking cussing some days
        I think how easy to finish what I started
    what I started to be the boss to write letters to let her
            let him work for me to promote him to

demote her to protect him to eject her to read
        of developmental needs of opportunities
    to be important portable skills from company to
            company portable like a lunch box

my four-year-old wants a Scooby-Doo lunch box
        maybe she can solve the mystery of the missing
    mother missing woman missing boss the mystery
            of the missing father

ONCE THE BOSS FIRED

Once the boss fired a twin the twin was torn in
        half at birth half the twin went to Human
Resources thinking they might be humane
        thinking they had resources for

the worker instead they had sorcery they laughed
        a cackling laugh they left her handed her a
layoff notice in an office poof tossed her out with
        a wand and three foot clicks went on

with their winding up firing denying benefits it's a
        benefit to have a job in America to have
a boss who gives you deploys you oils you
        when twins are born everyone says

congratulations the pink balloons come the pink blankets
        with the pink baboons arrive before noon
the twins will grow up and enter the world
        enter the workforce where they will

adjust to the dark learn how to duck when
        the light shines on their faces they
are still like us each time they are
        photographed they die a little more

THE BOSS HAS A DAUGHTER

The boss has a daughter the boss changes a diaper
   the boss tells us she is a successful woman
  the boss successes the boss confesses
    nothing the boss messes up if the boss

is a successful woman then what are we
    are we in trouble unable to reach treble
  unable to soar we are sore from bench pressing
    papers from leg pressing staples sour from

head-messes the boss has a daughter someone
    to care for the bus is powered by fuel the boss
  is powered by fools who are powered
    by the sun we have sons but they

are not old enough to save us they have no teeth yet
    we are powered by something like the son the
  corporation who is powered by the boss before
    the plane went down into the field someone

turned on all the storms in the sky before
    they stormed the cockpit the bosses
  saw the cars on the freeway driving to their offices they
    waved to the bosses in the cars but no one

saw them trapped behind the window once I taped up a hole
    of bees thousands in the dark dressed in their best
  black and yellow jackets I cried uncontrollably at
    night and wore stripes for the MRI

TODAY MY DAUGHTER

Today my daughter wants to be a waitress when she
        grows up she doesn't know that a waitress is
  not a boss that a waitress takes orders from everyone
       that a waitress must run to a bell to the

phone to the customer to the supervisor who is super
       bossy and wears a greasy visor
  yesterday my daughter wanted to be a pet doctor
       the Barbie book has fuzzy pets furry pets

cute pets with small noses Barbie doesn't show her
       missing finger from the cute pet that bit it off
  the Barbie is not the boss the dog is the boss Ken is
       the boss of the dog who likes the dog in a

pink outfit who likes Barbie in little skirts with little hips
       if a perfect woman like Barbie is not the boss then
  who can ever be the boss even the man in HR the man
       who can fire everyone cannot be the boss

because he has a boss who hired him who can fire
       him and even the man who hired the HR man
  has a boss who can fire him there are fires all over
       Japan right now the fire and water both want

to be the boss all the bosses in Japan lost their jobs
       lost their limbs bob in water no longer care
  about Bob the boss in America no longer
       care about cost

EDWARD HOPPER'S *OFFICE IN A SMALL CITY*

Maybe the man isn't looking out but he is
   looking down even his desk looks
  down on him his desk lies his desk tries to make
   him look busy but there are no stacks

of papers to make him sick the man
   and the desk have nothing they have a
  view with no people the man has no computer
   no keyboard to shoot words onto a

screen no keyboard that competes with the tap-tap
   of his heart the man has no spreadsheets
  with little rectangles filled with numbers the
   man is numb the man is

sitting in a building staring out of a rectangle
   from the front the building looks
  like a giant spreadsheet there would be
   thousands of rectangles

thousands of workers staring out like
   little numbers waiting to be shifted up
  shifted down summed up averaged
   deleted

THE BOSS CALLS US AT HOME

The boss calls us at home the boss can call us anytime
the boss tells us to turn on the television
not to go into work I watch over and over
the planes the buildings that met each

other wept each other the people stuck the boss's voice
shakes the boss must look familiar like a
mother like a sister but the boss isn't our mother isn't
our sister the shoe doesn't fit she can

whimper does whimper can feel sorry for other people
can vomit sadness when someone says
it's personal when is it not personal about the person
when the planes crashed into the

towers the pilots' bodies met a CEO their bodies
pressed together their power latched
together on the 54th floor hating each other embracing
each other like an accordion

ARE WE WRONG

Are we wrong yes we are wrong or yes
    we are wrong about being
      wrong does it really take two to tango or
        can a person tango by herself leg

twirling even a lift can be copied by jumping
      into the air but an abuser needs an
    obtuse one a victimizer needs a victim
      we are wrong the boss is

wrong the boss is right is height is higher
      than us on the ladder our fingers
    hurt our fingers are stepped on can someone
      be all right or all wrong

a tree is just a tree an ocean has salt a lake
      does not my father used to believe
    in black and white now he calls black
      white and white lack

THE BOSS IS A NO-FLY ZONE

The boss is a no-fly zone even when the boss
    misses numbers poor-performs even
    if the boss wears terrible perfume the boss is
        protected the boss's boss doesn't care the boss's

boss's boss works on his core at lunch on
    his chest on a bench the boss's boss's boss's
    boss thinks the boss does a fine job the boss
        jabs the workers trades barbs with

the workers the workers continue to do a fine job
    the boss's boss's boss just wants a fine
    job closes his outer lobe unless his son coughs
        like a sea at night

EDWARD HOPPER'S *CONFERENCE AT NIGHT*

The man sitting on the desk has no eyes or they
            are closed or they have been dug out
    the man sitting on the desk sits like a boss or
            perhaps he wants to be the boss and

the woman and man can help him the desks
            are bare except for two wooden boards
    they hold the man and shadows no papers no
            tacks no bored workers the man has

no stacks of anything the room can't be
            his office it's a morgue for
    people who have been *laid off fired sacked axed*
            let go why let go of the past why must

the past too be given a notice why can't
            we live in the past in our ugliest ruffle
    dresses the woman looks like a man maybe
            she will be a boss or maybe

it's better to look like a woman
            but act like a man a boss once told me
    never to act like a woman the woman
            stares beyond the man

the man on the desk is looking between
            the man and the woman whatever they are
    conferencing about has passed and everyone
            is still stressed

MY FATHER USED TO BE A BOSS

My father used to be a boss an office boss my father
       engineered his way up manager of a
    department fragment of a group of a fragment he departed
        with a gold plaque my father's office now

holds a different boss a different gold nameplate maybe
       ten bosses have gone through my father's office no one
   remembers him there the office remembers him
      its walls know the voice of a Chinese

man who wanted to be boss for his daughter to be
      boss for his lost daughter to be bought by
   a corporation his daughter cannot boss does not
      want to boss prefers to be bossed to be

last to lust after a good boss I do I don't I do not I don't
      what is it that I want that I don't want that wants
  me that doesn't want me my daughter stands
     at the window her tears can still open

her face like a zipper she knows exactly what she wants
      she wants to play with the eleven-year-old who
  no longer has time to play with her who is busy on
     her path to becoming a boss

I AM AFRAID TO BE AFRAID

I am afraid to be afraid too afraid
        to be me of what will happen if you open
    this box of me for the boss to see that
        I am afraid of the boss that we

are lost my father is lost my father
        is afraid of himself afraid
    of us afraid to talk my father says the wrong
        things my two-year-old says

the wrong things *him not here him go work*
        me not have juice me not have father
    my father used to be president used to be present
        used to present slides in front of people

I used to accept his presents after business trips
        I used to be afraid of my father I used
    to get tokens to play Ms. Pac-Man for As
        used to win Ms. Pac-Man now

I am afraid of the blue ghosts the green
        and orange ghosts I am afraid to eat
    the white pellets white poisonous pellets if I eat
        them all I will get to the 256th level

that level is unplayable has a bug when summer
        finally arrives I am scared because
    the flies come with their compound
        eyes that see everything

EDWARD HOPPER'S *OFFICE AT NIGHT*

The man isn't paying bills isn't invoicing isn't
        lowering his voice the man is
the boss preparing for performance evaluations
           for tomorrow this round is a big one he has

forty-two to deliver to beggars Kelly's *attitude is*
        an asset Jim *starts and ends meetings on time*
    Polly is an *effective communicator* Jenny is a *team player*
        but Jenny has difficulty *thinking*

outside the box Jenny is locked inside her cubicle
        Jenny can't stop snacking on Cheez-Its
Jenny hates the boss the boss encourages her to
        develop solutions the boss is at

a loss the boss's boss hates the boss the boss's
        boss hired but now can't fire the boss
it's too much work to toss the boss the woman in
        the blue dress likes Jenny is friends with

Jenny speaks up for Jenny sparks arc from her
        evaluation the boss will fire her too she will walk
out the blue door in her blue dress get paid less
        the door will close will lose its shadow

I HAVE A NEW BOSS

I have a new boss a new house a new old house
    too tired to boss us an old lady lived
  here handicap bars everywhere as if she knew
      I needed them to hold me up to help me stand

my two-year-old trips on everything I no longer
    trip on everything the woman who used to live here
  was named Thelma Thelma is an old person's name a nice
      person's name maybe Thelma was a nice boss

the man across the street is ninety-four his wife
    doesn't leave the house on some sunny days I see
  a shadow in a wheelchair sitting behind the screen
      door he carries a walkie-talkie she beeps him

bosses him the woman next door is eighty-eight
    her husband's name is Arthur Miller
  he's never written a play never played
      a Marilyn but instead a Barbara who

is the boss of Halloween who gives out pencils instead
    of candy all our neighbors used to have bosses
  used to be bosses used to be nice bosses or cruel
      bosses now they breathe they prepare to leave

EDWARD HOPPER'S *AUTOMAT*

The woman in the automat doesn't know about
    the earthquake doesn't worry about
  the earthquake in Japan another earthquake
      in Japan she will be dead by the time the

earthquake comes again she is gone by the time the
    earthquake comes again she can't be a boss looks
  too nice to be a boss she looks Japanese she
    could be a boss why does it

matter she is gone the boss doesn't matter
    anymore the boss doesn't make us
  anymore there's an earthquake in Japan again the water
    follows the theories of power the water

takes what it wants the water doesn't want
    what it wants but takes it anyway the
  children's book the old photo the couple
    having sex on the roof the people want the

water to leave the people have no power they want
    power the people are on the roof
  of the building the people are no longer on
    the roof of the building

THANKS

Thank you to the editors of the following journals in which many of the poems in this book appeared, often in earlier forms: *Agni, American Poetry Review, Believer, Blackbird, Colorado Review, Gulf Coast, Kenyon Review, The Margins, Missouri Review, New England Review, Ploughshares, Poetry Daily, Smartish Pace, Taos Journal of Poetry & Art, Tin House, Threepenny Review,* and *Virginia Quarterly Review.* Thanks also to *At Length* and Wave Books for republishing several of these poems.

I will always have fond memories of multiple marathon four-hour Skype sessions with Dominic Luxford and Jesse Nathan while we worked passionately on this manuscript. Editors like them who read, re-read, and read again intelligently, happily, and selflessly are hard to find. Thanks also go out to the whole McSweeney's team for their vision and hard work.

Because working as a poet can be isolating, thank you to all of my friends and supporters, old and new—there are too many to mention here.

Thank you to my family and especially to my future little bosses, Penny and Winnie.

ABOUT THE AUTHOR

Victoria Chang's two previous collections of poetry are *Salvinia Molesta*, published by the University of Georgia Press as part of the VQR Poetry Series in 2008, and *Circle*, published by the Southern Illinois University Press as the winner of the Crab Orchard Open Competition in 2005. Her poems appear in the *Believer, Poetry, American Poetry Review, Kenyon Review, Virginia Quarterly Review, Tin House, New England Review, Colorado Review, Smartish Pace, Blackbird*, and elsewhere. She holds degrees from the University of Michigan, Harvard, and Stanford, as well as an MFA from Warren Wilson. She works in business and lives in Southern California with her family.

THE M^cSWEENEY'S POETRY SERIES

THE
M^cSWEENEY'S POETRY SERIES

The McSweeney's Poetry Series is founded on the idea that good poems can come in any style or form, by poets of any age anywhere. Our goal is to publish the best, most vital work we can find, regardless of pedigree. We're after poems that move, provoke, inspire, delight— poems that tear a hole in the sky. And when we find them, we'll publish them the only way we know how: in beautiful hardbacks, with original artwork on the cover. These are books to own, books to cherish, books to loan to friends only in rare circumstances.

>>> —— <<<

SUBSCRIPTIONS

The McSweeney's Poetry Series subscription includes our next four books for only $40—an average of $10 per book—delivered to your door, shipping included. You can sign up at store.mcsweeneys.net

>>> —— <<<

PREVIOUS TITLES

Love, an Index by Rebecca Lindenberg
"An A-to-Z collection of poems that are passionate, plainspoken, elegiac, and lyric as they capture the moments of a life shared."   —*Vanity Fair*

Fragile Acts by Allan Peterson
"Like 'Brazil's undiscovered caverns of amethyst,' Allan Peterson's *Fragile Acts* is a major find."   —John Ashbery

City of Rivers by Zubair Ahmed
"When reading Zubair Ahmed I feel as though I am both witnessing and taking part in an ecstatic, lyric experience."   —Matthew Dickman

x by Dan Chelotti
"Dan Chelotti's poems spin and jump through fire landing on their feet … a poet with grace and beauty in his duffle bag."   —James Tate